A WHOLE DAY
THROUGH FROM
WAKING

JACCI BULMAN

INDEPENDENT INNOVATIVE INTERNATIONAL

Published by Cinnamon Press,
Meirion House,
Tanygrisiau
Blaenau Ffestiniog,
Gwynedd,
 LL41 3SU
www.cinnamonpress.com
The right of Jacci Bulman to be identified as author of this work
has been asserted by her in accordance with the Copyright,
Designs and Patent Act, 1988. Copyright © 2016 Jacci Bulman.
ISBN: 978-1-910836-27-9
British Library Cataloguing in Publication Data. A CIP record for
this book can be obtained from the British Library.

Designed and typeset in Palatino by Cinnamon Press. Printed in
Poland. Cover design by Adam Craig

Cinnamon Press is represented in the UK by Inpress Ltd
www.inpressbooks.co.uk and in Wales by the Welsh Books
Council www.cllc.org.uk

Acknowledgements

Extract from the poem 'Verdi' by Charles Bukowski, from *Pleasures of the Damned*, first published by Ecco, an imprint of HarperCollins in 2007. Published by Canongate Books Ltd in the United Kingdom in 2010. © copyright Linda Bukowski, 2007. Used with permission.

For previous publication of early versions of these poems, thanks to: Cinnamon Press, *Feeding the Cat* 2011, *A Roof of Red Tiles* 2011, *In Terra Pax* 2012, *The Book of Euclid* 2013; *The New Writer*, 109, 2012; *Other Poetry* Series 4 No 5, 2012; *Domestic Cherry* 2, 2012; *Acumen*, 72, 2012 and 80, 2014; *Obsessed with Pipework*, 59, 2012; Flarestack Poets anthology *Sylvia is Missing* 2012; *Fire Crane* 02, 2012; *Fourteen*, 14, 2012; Mirehouse WBTW Poetry Competition 2012 and 2014, *Iota*, 92, 2013; *Third Way*, Dec 2013; *Envoi*, 166, 2013; Indigo Dreams Press, (*Saraswati* 034), *The North*, 52, 2014, *Agenda*, online supplement, vol 48 nos 3-4, *The Way*, winter issue 2014, *The Rialto*, 85, 2016,

Thanks also to Brigid Rose, for her long-standing critical support; to my family and Niki, for being in my life; to Lindsay, for still being; to Simon, for his light; to my editor Jan, for her patience and connection; to Eden Poets, for their valuable feedback; and to Khanh, Van Mai, Anh, Sen, Ly, Phuc, Hien, Vu, Hanh, Yen Nhi and Jackie, in Vietnam – together we founded The Kianh Foundation: www.kianh.org.uk

Contents

For Alan, my sky

love –
it can and should be so
easy
like falling asleep
in a chair or
like a church full of
windows

from 'Verdi' by Charles Bukowski

Happiness in the ordinary sense is not what one needs in life, though one is right to aim at it. The true satisfaction is to come through and see those whom one loves come through.

E.M. Forster
Selected Letters, letter 216, to Florence Barger,
11th Feb. 1916

A Whole Day Through
From Waking

The Big Exhibition Room

Four Choices of Story
says the sign.
I choose the piece of labradorite.
She tells me an Inuit folk-tale
of Northern Lights
being trapped inside:
how a warrior's spear
did not free them.
And I think of my own stones,
at home on the dusty window-sill:
stash of imprisoned sky.

She lets me pick another.
I go for a grey rock
millions of years old.
Hold the fossil like I once held
           birthday gifts:
anticipation the greatest part.

Having captured me
she fills with blood,
her eyes alive
along with every object
in the room. For seconds
nothing in the world is dead.

We called her Julie

She was the pink-orange light
on the corrugated factory-roof,
around a vent emitting vapours
from the slipper-works.

Most nights we felt compelled
to stand beneath the chestnut trees
on Windsor Road, above the park,
salute her.

I showed Wendy how:
one arm stretched high,
looking towards the factory,
we chanted, *Hail Julie.*

It was a ritual to emphasise
our earthliness; hopeful
of what might help us
if we both showed deference.

Occasionally I find her again,
not in trees or bracken
or the river-bed, but in the sheen on wings,
in the unbranded maverick.

After I wet my knickers

We are in the Tranny driving back to his dad's farm
and I'm pressing my thighs together.
He's oblivious to how I'm trying to carry my whole weight
on my feet, so that nothing of me touches the upholstery.

I have never wanted a journey to pass so fast,
next to him. Every other has been me trying to speak
without licking dry lips; to listen without needing
to repeat the word *Pardon?*

I pat the dog's head. We make a fast swerve
and I am tipped towards him.
Pray for a vacuum to suck up
the smell of me.

Age 13: just learning

At night I heard the rhythms
of her bed, fell asleep to the back
and forth of her and him.

In the mornings she came down
with a thick clump of matted hair—
everyone in the kitchen laughed.

Over breakfast she was rosy faced
and between them I caught smiles
that bound them,

like raiders of heaven.

But what I remember most
was her house: the first place I'd seen
that was not clean.

On the stairs hair, thick balls of dust
you could pick up.
I took it all in—

her house, her smile,
her bowls of ripe plums,
vases full of blue delphiniums.

A Touch of Rouge

Always perfect co-ordinates:
colour themes of red jazz or lemon Easter,
black mask to match the cowboy hat.
When I see her at the bus-stop —
wild blue feather boas and pom-pom ponchos,
sequined specs and dicky-bows,
the wait jumps like a giant leap-frog.

The man who lives in the next-door flat
walks the supermarket aisles, sits at the theatre
in heels and rouge, lace petticoat peeking
from his skirt hem. A silver hair-slide.
And those eyes, daring anyone to snitch on him,
break the spell of pretend.

Fascinated by the dipping-duck,
the secret liquid in the pot; the kiss of Beauty.

On past Bethesda

We hitch-hiked through Wales
towards the WOMAD festival,
me with a Brazilian drum—
red and long as my legs—
given a lift by the man from
'Porridge', a thin sweep of hair
across the top of his head,
the man who loved to talk, loved
Wales more, took us on a tour
of the best bits, dropped us off
out of his way, and we found
a field, camped by a stone barn,
went round the side in the black dark
and made love against a wall, the moon
absent, the cows asleep in the field,
stones warm and flat
against my back.

We didn't try to work it out,
life, didn't think of anything except
where we could next make love.
Till one day you needed more,
needed to pull reality apart.
And we never found a wall again,
that absence of the moon.

visit the open unit

his eyes bloodshot me looking into one
at a time asking for the sphinx to move

kissing the taste of drink of drugs tasting me
near numb remembering I feel nothing
if not our last real kiss his empty mouth

I wait on the underneath the back of a well
for an opening to appear   pulling away

from his hand I offer my hip the edge of it
offer a piece of me to see
if he is here

me only wanting to stroke his hair soft
his hair freshly washed clean our dirty rain
biting my own lip for being here

closing his eyes I disappear
as his hand stops moving we breathe out

we disappear a forest moss raspberries
kiss his eyelids his face lets go of grief
as the lines of his eyes droop towards sleep

kiss his eyelids kiss parachute skin

Not Enough

I can get right to our first kiss, lying by a waterfall cliff
in Glen Affric, when we almost crushed your glasses as we
rolled on the ground; nearly fell over the edge.

The time you left me in a clearing by the raspberry bushes,
found me again by my penny-whistle playing;
two love-drunk pixies.

The morning you met me after Skye, when your eyes looked
like you were burning inside, but we still found fusion;
wildly ecstatic.

Bring back that day when I found you in Edinburgh
with slashed wrists, had to bandage them,
cover up, keep quiet, speak to you calmly while I spun.

Easy to have you in my living room,
scaring me a little with the way you spoke;
not knowing what in God's name to do.

I can summon us, sitting on a park bench in Elgin,
talking about why roses are different colours.
Me saying they just are, you insisting there must be a reason.

I can touch the jealousy when I brought you a sunflower
on the ward, and you went on about that other girl,
who told you not to take your medicine.

Where I was, in a car at the supermarket,
being told what you'd done.
Standing on the bridge where you'd jumped,

throwing a rose: questioning my part.
An image of a rescue-helicopter hovering above.
You refusing; arms beating the river.

But I can't trace the shape of your neck,
feel the heat from your hand in mine,
your breath as we lay behind sand dunes.

I can't catch the dreams we had, the taste of your lips,
the sound of your laugh. And the idea that there is
more than this, is not enough.

I couldn't tell if the woman's words were upsetting me

or if I was telling myself to be upset.

The woman from Penrith began
with a poem by Pam Ayres.
She was good. Even got the accent.

Then, after one about apple trees in autumn,
she started a piece about drowning.
It was half-way between farce and facts,
quotes from a book written in 1832 —
how to resuscitate the nearly-drowned.

Everyone chuckled.

Lines about scrubbing the body with horse-hair mittens,
putting it in a hot bath,
pumping the lungs with a tube
to bring back breath

and flashing between her words,
calling me like a dog in the woods, was you.

I didn't know if I should look down,
walk out, light a cigarette,
if I should stand up, protest
or if this was just me being O.T.T.

The audience continued to laugh
and your hands reached out from the river
as if, at last,
you had decided to come back.

My grief, now you ask

is the space between veins on the wings of a fly
as it lands on the leaf of a sycamore tree,

is electrons shooting luminescence
down a cathode tube to make a movie.

Miniscule

as an ant I can fold my fingers around,
the handle on a doll's house tea-cup.

I can hold it, just.

Nothing like an iceberg or a rhinoceros, no.

It is almost big enough to fill a dandelion seed
—waiting to be blown—

In Turkish groves near Paphos

A long valley of them,
big and ripe,
declarations hanging
from untended trees.
Walking through where
momentum has fled,
and in every swollen fruit,
an asking.
We do not want to shout
or laugh, as if mirth
has drained from the land,
and the only remaining brightness
lies in oranges.

Casa Borboleta

How sharp is the flick of love
I feel for you? For your fallen walls
and lack of road? But no, not that.
For your bread oven, stone bees,
neglected grapes? None of these, none.
For the spring water tap on a slate path
where water drips? Not this.
To describe you, my love?
As much a swift drenching
as a downpour of arrows.

noon in the stable

stroke them both at the temples
small fingertip circles
first P then Blue lets go
heads down   eyes twitch   close
muzzles rest
in my curled elbows
slide heavy into sleep   trust
I stand their weight
as both drop deeper
hold my body still
think *amazing* and then
as every time before
I want to stop something beautiful
before something beautiful is stopped
and I go

Curtains

Now the only thing I need
is a lambswool jumper, pink,

crew necked —
not so tight it suffocates.

Lambswool in case it gets
too cold over winter

but acrylic would do —
I shan't be going out much.

In fact I'll be here where I am now,
sitting on my sofa with golden cushions

and the heating will be on —
not too high to make me weary

but I dislike the cold:
no, no, that's too depressing.

Last month I looked through the brochure,
had a search for my jumper

but fashion doesn't seem to be very pink this year —
except a gaudy type, cerise.

So I ordered a new green skirt
which I don't really need

and when it arrived it matched my curtains.
I think that's quite sad,

the way I'm beginning to look like my house.

Hanoi Cocktail

Her hair swings as she moves.
Old wooden tables painted black; tall stools.
Whiskies and cognacs in two lines
arranged by shape;
lights shining through glass.

The letters 'Bols- Blu-' and a turquoise liquid
above faded stencils of horses; Chinese scrawl.
Above my head a TV shows deep-sea photography:
orange corals; a commentary in German.

Three men play cards at the bar; slap down their turns.
Another walks in, whacks his friend on the backside;
looks at me and passes.
In the back kitchen someone chops fast onto a board
while outside cyclo-boys pedal back and
forth, hunting for fares.

Music comes on halfway through *'Careless Whisper'*.
I hang there until the song is drowned
by a blending-machine.

The glass collector combs her locks slowly, slowly
on the step outside:
the egg-shell décor of the comb;
her thin fingers;
the mark near her throat.

I sit until I can't stand my empty glass,
get up, head back to the hotel,
feeling followed by

the lack of you.

Meal Out

from Hoi An Orphanage, Vietnam

We're eating big prawns.
I peel the shells off, swallow
soft bodies, the easy pulp.

The boy next to me lingers,
gets into the skulls and
threads of flesh on legs
before crunching skeletons,
his and mine. We laugh.

He comes from a hill tribe, I learn,
where newborn babies are buried
with mothers who die giving birth.
He was dug out.

We sit at that table
eating prawns,
trying to talk about football,
like we're a stretched out concertina,
the same air between us.

Valiant

for Van Mai, Hoi An Orphanage, Vietnam

A monarch butterfly
migrating south,
flying thousands of miles

up high,
assisted only by wind.

And you,
walking.

Hard

for Anh, Hoi An Orphanage, Vietnam

Curled up, blind, on a shared bed,
facing the boards,
you beat your head on them.
At first I can't approach you:
your tiny curve terrifies,
with its rhythmic efforts to cancel life.
But when the man comes to shave your head,
pulls it over the edge of the bed
and leaves you screaming,
I cannot do nothing.
And your empty eyes,
sealed up, spattered with shaven hairs,
unfasten me.

*

I hold you, on a bus-trip,
I watch you feel the wheels move.
Your smile engulfs me.

*

You're whizzing in a toddler-walker
around the yard:
loving those wheels.

Bumping into walls,
sometimes stuck in a corner,
people rarely help,
but you never give up.

*

Time on,
all assistance removed,
you are back on a hard bed.

Your face
as you felt good movement:
how unthinkable now
the diminution.

War Crimes

At twenty, she is taken from her orphanage bed
to the War Crimes Shelter
(it's where they go, post age eighteen;
it's where she will stay).

She laughs
as they carry her in,
her body a plank of wood
that won't un-stiffen.

No children on beds next to her.
No visiting tourists who'll paint her nails—
bring her a National Geographic
with pictures of sea, houses, trees.

She is in a room with Agent Orange adults:
one lady with a gentle face and one blind mad woman
who beats the nits in her hair with a slipper.

Hien lies in her shelter for poisoned people,
finds things to laugh over,
waits, while outside
tourists walk to their favourite restaurants.

Khanh

He points to who hasn't had a biscuit yet;
squats in the yard to watch other kids playing football;
watches us all.

He can't walk or talk,
sing or dance,
but somehow looks like he could do all of these
and more,
or none of it and still laugh.

What I see in him,
like the big answer on a rice grain,
is forgiveness.

He has somehow forgiven
God, the world, his country, his family,
the workers who treat him
like cheap meat,
tourists like me
who try to make him their souvenir,
forgiven us all,
and for that

he has gained something
I can't get into focus,
but it is grace.

Khanh inspired us to name The Kianh Foundation in his honour –
a charity for children with disabilities in Vietnam, www.kianh.org.uk

Graffiti with love
for Arthur Stace

Up above is your word again: 'ETERNITY'.
'Eternity' over Sydney Harbour Bridge.
'Eternity' half a million times chalked
onto pavements around the city.

Scribbled with intent at just gone 5 a.m.
at the feet of tower-blocks,
around shops and bus-stops
for when the rushing world wakes up.

Eternal thanks that you're no longer
living rough and drunk and thieving.
Eternal devotion to what you found
promised in Isaiah 57, verse15.

You, who for three decades and more
gave graffiti to your city with love,
were forgiven your dusty call to 'Eternity'
blazoning now as fireworks in the sky.

This poem was written in honour of a man whose continuous graffiti word 'Eternity' was made into a huge firework display - styled in his handwriting - at the Sydney 2000 celebrations.

There's a small crowd around him now

His whiskers,
his fingers on the banjo,
loud notes filling the road,
they catch us like loom-hooks.
The sheep-dog by his side
howls when he nods
and we all want to be that close—
his voice and eyes shuttling through
on a line that has snuck between us.
And we all stand, nudged inches in,
forgetting anything but warmth.

Hands in jacket pockets

An evening beach, us two
in the purple-dark;
grey sea, barely visible stones
between streams that meander.
I step onto the soft mounds
as you peer amongst rocks for treasure,
then – stood upright,
you look out into the night.
I watch your thin strip of life,
blurred edges, no specific details,
and know how small we are,
how much our passing will be
as sea-foam disappears into sand ripples,
but tonight we are bigger than the sky.

A call to say if you have something terrible

In the midst of playing
at getting life right
I spend the afternoon
waiting
for a phone call

that could jerk us into another
everything: where jam tastes different,
where putting your boots by the door
is a hold on tomorrow,
and planning a holiday
is some fantasy.

Now the rest of the day is scenery
through the window of a time-machine.
It's hurtling past —
outlines merging slowly into a grip
that hurts the mind.

I feel no gravity,
no wind on the face.
Only split matter.

Held

Her purple skirt pinched between fingers,
she takes his words:
cannot wait another day.
Words that should have been
it worked.

No time to argue the difference between this
and what was promised —
was it promised?

She stands up, walks around the crowded room,
shakes every hand.
Thank-you, she tells them all. *Thank-you.*
Seems the most appropriate word at the time.
So stupid later.

Walks out into the coffee room next door.
The liaison officer follows her;
a blur of purple.

This heaven thing

We walk along the roadside to kill time.
You're fascinated by the way that water runs
so fast –
down the road then disappears.

Where does it go?
You want to know.

Leaning on a gate, looking at hills,
horizon, sky,
I close my eyes,
feel the earth swing.

And I want to turn what we've found
upside down,
shake it out for holes
and hidden fouls,
because it's not forever,
this killing time.

And death is more outrageous now,
even more so,
         even more.

Decoy

A risky operation—
the blood-swollen birth-mark
on her daughter's head—
no surgeon across Europe
had dared to remove it,
until now.

Bizarre then, you could say,
that she found relief in the evenings
by ridiculing other patients:

a young girl with
no front to her face—
two sides joined along an edge—
a *tropical fish*.

And us, staying for six weeks,
praying for grace,
she had to report us
for kissing on the sofa,
leaving leaves in the tea-pot.

I didn't understand, then—
a mother yelling inside,
needing to trip the rest of us up.
Any chance of distraction.

This isn't a horror

It's the Tate Modern,
a day out
after a clear scan.
And it's walking wide corridors
to discover weird art.

On a slope upwards
to another floor
a man stops me politely,
to ask if he could ask me a favour—

could he please take my photograph?
He doesn't say why but I know
and want him to say it,
but in the end I have to.

Yes, he says, *that's true,*
but it's not what you think.
I want to show someone can be beautiful
while also disfigured,
and I blush.

I'm a professional, he says,
I'll pay you,
so I say, *yes, okay*
and he takes me to various walls,
alcoves

serious poses and then,
like a model, on the lawn,

and I feel as much like I'm in a film
as I do when I lie inside a scanner,
only slightly more up-beat.

The judgement surely fragile

We were given a name,
a label for what you had
but now it is faded.
I have days when I know the cure—
the closest to a cure, at least—was
waiting as a quiet thing waits.
From the alcove, or on the ward,
your sallow face slacker, gaunt,
looking at your boots
or to a horizontal sky,
no power to ask but we could
have asked it of ourselves.
When the chalk was taken from you
and we held it—
red chalk sweaty in our hands—
we could have slipped it back, somehow,
for you to draw your own way out.

on the tip very close

Thistledown—
she heard the word and needed to repeat it
several times, especially the '*-istle*', it brought memories of
Beatrix Potter, which were not really memories but
fantasies of a childhood never quite, almost,
—*and isn't that just what thistledown is?* she thought,
a feeling of nearly, of travelling 'back there', as you walk
by a big seed thistle, pull off its head, apologise, then
wallow soft in the texture between your fingers, like the
satin ribbon on the edge of an old woollen blanket, or
the label on one particular chiffon blouse, rubbed slow
between finger and thumb, then there's the sliding of palm
along twisted rope, of lead-reins, even tree-swings—
something touched before she was born.

A Victorian nightgown

hangs
        from the rafters
of this Norwich antique shop

more than thirty years
        ago,
still now,

hand-made yellow lace
        edging a
hem, collar, cuffs,

white cotton
        shone through
by light,

and still the wish to
        take it down,
billow it

in an outside street,
        keen air
within—

a white goose
        ready
to take flight.

Theft

Four young calves in a field.
Not such a sunny day, yet the sun.

Necks arched back in crescent stretches
to keep their faces in the warm.

All four of them in the same position
to hold balance, just.

*

Night. The mother cows in the field near the church
are bawling a hellish sound.
I try to sleep.

2 a.m. More cows:
a deep bellied call that stammers my heart.

Their calves are gone.
They beseech the sky for their return.

I lie awake,
shake with shame for what we do.

please come away

Last night I walked the river path,
found you, night-warming: eggs still blank.
You turned up this morning at the yard, looking scrawny.
By the time I'd fed the stock, you were gone.
I wanted to tell you in a way you'd understand:
the chicks aren't coming.

*

Brought food to put near you this evening
at your nest in the reeds: as usual
you pretended not to see me—
head bobbed down to concentrate on huddling.

*

Over weeks, odd days, an egg disappears, fox-taken,
till one is left, and you still sit in hope.
You're getting thin, not learning.
I wait till you go scratching for food up the yard,
take your last egg, hold it in my palm.

Swan's Egg

The collection is held in a fine granite house,
gifted to the people: it retains the pleasures
of being lived in.
Whilst browsing the costumes
I'm thinking of the walled garden
we visited earlier—meeting the owner there,
with her dogs:

being in awe that she would so gladly share
her place with the public,
not for profit
but for them to sit on a bench and breathe in
the scents; see the bees on the white flowers.

We go into a room with a new exhibition
of clothes worn by Land Girls and Lumber Jills:
a dress made from a sofa cover;
a coat, big to allow plenty of movement;
a handbag made to fit a gas mask neatly;
and this swan's egg.

On it are the signatures
of the team of men and women
who worked at Auchlossen Drainage Scheme,
near Aberdeen.

Held and signed by Edith Taylor, Peter Martin,
James and Daisy Davidson…
when the task set before them was done.
Perhaps over a spot of drink,
laughter.

And I suppose afterwards
someone blew out the insides of the egg,
making it even more fragile,
but it still held.

Jesus on the wall

I'd love to go to my favourite church
and let him down,
shake loose his arms,
watch him have a runabout
before they put him back.

I want to fly to mountain bars above Gois,
hide in nooks till just before dawn,
open the doors of metal cages
where café owners keep canaries,

listen as owners rise for chores—
wonder what is missing.

One bird might stay,
loyal, confined,
to stop the silence shaking them.

An Accrington Education

You were the only one I ever dared show my warts—
kept serene as I twined on
about different ways to kill them.

In biology you were my bench-mate—
a gatepost that held me steady
when I felt like flapping in the wind.

But then we did evolution.
You began to cry, became petrified—
sure you'd be cast out, punished,

even for listening. I knew
you were a 'born-again'. How much you enjoyed
your full-dunk baptism; the happy singing.

But it's not RIGHT, it's not right!
you repeated, eyes wanting to
flee the room; your cheeks wet through.

I sat and observed but didn't give you
any steadiness that day; didn't hold you.
I wish I had told you *your miracle story,*

your Adam-and-Eve of it,
they are still an ingredient,
in this cauldron of unlikely truths.

Cumberland Infirmary Dermatology Unit, 1pm

Last night we watched a film,
you stroked my feet,
we ate peppermint creams,
every few minutes I remembered,
you remembered,
then I made pictures behind my eyes —
us on top of Saddleback mountain,
me reading at a book launch,
and I prayed,
like you only pray when you are
afraid.

In the early hours when we
woke up, you stroked my back,
I prayed more,
uttered *I ask, I ask,* then added
I trust I trust, until I wasn't sure
which came first — or if you can have
both together.
Said my request
then added my surrender.

Tonight we'll watch a film,
drink wine, I'll say you can
hold me, and you might,
we'll watch *Under Milk Wood*
and criticise the director.

Tomorrow I'll clean the house,
with all the time in the world.

Evening after a disaster at work

The fat tadpoles are a relief.
She peers down
at their attempts to grab pond-weed,
new legs taking a rest on submerged reed.

The mud nearby is leaking
oil into the water—
bits break off the blob, disperse
translucent polygons across the surface.

A few new frogs
have ventured onto the top
of corrugated tin
laid down to offer shelter.

Their thin skin sticks to the metal
in summer's heat.
Two are dead.
Another is trying to wrench free.

Its body loose but a leg trapped,
she slides a reed beneath and,
in a second it leaps
into water.

She sits on a log, watches rain
break the skin of the pond—
hopes the plastic bottle tied to a pole
will keep the heron away.

It's further than we thought

along this limb of land called Foulney Island,
we're heading for the end but we can't see it—
        the wind blows a gale,
my fingers yellow-white numb;
there are hardly any birds on this reserve.

You want to reach the conclusion
and I want you to be happy, so we keep on:
        lean into the wind.

A man-made breakwater in the middle of the strip
we tread like a slippy aeroplane runway,
parts of it broken away, fallen into the pebbles below,
making us unsure which path is best; we change our minds
depending on the slipperiness.

My fingers can take no more. I hide
behind some concrete-mixed-with-rock
of this broken breakwater: a handy tent
to keep the wind off me, while you head to the tip.

        I wait, huddled under concrete,
watch all the birds I notice now, dipping into sand.

        Time here, on these stones,
to be alone with this;
move it inside my ribs, try to shake it out,
        absorb—perhaps a hair's width.

        I'm glad when you come back
and we set off to the mainland,
our green car in the distance—
        heavy rain arrives,
chucks down on us and I laugh,
we'd be dry if we'd headed back sooner!
but we both know that wasn't meant, this day,

and the tide's coming in,
it's moving feet-fast towards us,
to cover our peninsula, drown us in a flash—
        I'm afraid. Not of the sea but of my cells.
We hold hands and laugh as if
we face the maverick,
        dance before it.

These seconds are honey on warm bread

I sit and wait for the washing-machine dial to move
from 'stop' to 'release', so I can open the door, pull out clothes—
no obligation in this pause to do anything more.

Dirt around the skirtings of the room,
dust-clumps like tumbleweed,
drift about when any breeze lifts them.
Mixtures of feather, hair, essential blue fluff.

A torn piece of cardboard on top of the machine,
the word 'dirty' written on it in blue felt-tip—
left-over from bags of laundry now all part of the pile
in the spare room.

The red light on the door clicks off.
Extra moments on the step:
through the gap in the skylight the blackbird,
singing to the valley.

Beyond, the river runs by, the sheep on the hill
bleat and dash as the farmer arrives on his tractor.
Winter hay. The last few weeks of it.

She reads *The Art of Happiness* on the bus

then listens to two young girls talk about tattoos.

Thinks she doesn't love a man over and over,
then realises she knows nothing truer than that love.

O! And the banality, so nearly grasped, of searching for anything
other than a pack of hula-hoops.

Madison County
after the film

That certainty, once in your life if you're lucky —
that's what he said, and I knew immediately
what he meant.

Look at you.
Try to add up the ire we've had between us,
times you've pinched the quick of me, flippantly,
me having to keep striking matches.

But it doesn't count.
I look and cannot make this force inside me quaver,
cannot diminish it,
not even with all the blown lights.

Still that certainty,
like a block of blue swept across the canvas —
this is my sky.

Paint

In your hands two makeshift newspaper plugs
used to stop holes in the window frame
where sash-cords used to go.

A spider lives in there, you say.
Sometimes see him looking about for flies.
Thought it best to keep him inside.

I picture you yesterday,
at the window frame, ready to paint,
shutting a spider in, just to be safe

(you when the world isn't looking)
and I know we have the best hope
of coming out of this unbroken.

It's a pair of trapeze artists
in Billy Smart's Circus

It's a stinker of a day. Ring you at work
        only to say
we need shopping on your way home,
manage to pick a fight about
        a lemon.
Is the one in the fridge – half squeezed –
        enough? You don't understand,
I'm making fish pie!

Nothing like the day between us when we went looking round
        a big
deserted granite house, kidding ourselves we could bid for it,
imagining what to do with all the scullery rooms, the
        huge hallway,
running our hands across marble fireplaces,
down
        walnut banisters, nothing like that today.

Or like the time we looked at an old Scottish cottage down a
        two-mile track,
deep in pine plantation, and we walked around the marsh-land
hoping to see an adder or a grass-snake, talked about
        what we'd do next.

Today I'm just cooped up in bed, with a bad back and
when I phone you I'm a grump
when I'd wanted to say you looked good this morning,
in your blue shirt,
but we have something now we
        didn't have then,
something I'd rather not call love.

Give it a new name, just for today, a fanfare
to brighten the stale air in here, paint the walls with—
        a flamenco orange—
let it dangle from the ceiling—a purple feather dragon puppet,
        dancing across.
No—open the window and let it
        loose into the sky,
because I know it has a home,

this thing that shivers but never leaves,
is the bearer of close cruelties,
and usher of heaven's uplift.

A whole day through from waking —

allowing love.

Halt has been called,
by whom? we forget.
It came like a heron to the river.

My bitch is set free,
(barked as far as Mars,
bit the air like a jackal).
His rats are scattered.

Now we sit quiet by the water,
he watches the deep pool for fish,
I look at his lips and
watch only that part of him.

On a site set back from the estuary

She's hanging washing
from her caravan window:
the old lady neighbour walks by.
They talk about summer coming,
the dogs last night, how Helen Fraser
is doing in California, then,
as she goes, the lady tells her
You have nothing to do in this life, love.
You are enough. And is gone.

She carries on placing T- shirts and
socks on the rail, looks up at the sky,
around the site, to see if someone
heard, or could explain. But there's
only the birds on the telegraph wire
above her, singing.

Sonnet to joy

The sea crashes and says he can
throw rocks into her foam,
the sky calls out no-one will see
if he wants to rage into her airy expanse,
yell at the clouds,
but just when the taste of it
has soaked into his bones,
when his tissues know,
his blood knows, he will end,
a new happiness comes,
like the fool at the tragedy
but the lucky fool,

whose acceptance of death
makes him rejoice beyond time.

Two Days

until the flight back.
Builders paid, sale put through.
Everything else can be left
undone.

Walking the forests alone,
up through eucalyptus trees.
The few birds.
Stony paths.

Two days of something—
can't remember the feeling,
how to recall joy,
in exactium?

When she tries, she sees a girl walking
a mountain track,
legs longer than hers,
walking on
beams.

In these few hours of no questioning

The journey here involved a donkey-cart,
the two of us walking across scrubland
to relieve the donkey.

The Dogon homes are baked earth.
We are shown around, served our favourite—
delicious chicken in a peanut sauce,
at a hyped up price.
Plus cool-box Coca-Cola.
The evening we spend with some local boys,
listening to Tracy Chapman on a ghetto-blaster.

How my friend looks:
red dust on her face,
wisps of hair blowing around her pony-tail,
her lilac T-shirt faded by weeks of hot sun.

We climb onto the roof of a home
to sleep on our Karrimats,
each on a blue cocoon sleeping bag.

Dogon people
we can hear chatting and listening to music below;
insects drone.

We sit cross-legged for a while
to stare at the cliffs

It happened fast

he was staring at me as we made love,
watching me, the woman he married,

when I chose, very briefly, to look into his eyes,
stare back,

then, without intention, fell in—
it's the only way to put it—

I fell right into his body,
as if the soul does not only reside

in its vehicle,
but can move to other places, as it did—

my spirit dived through his eyes,
dark now as narrow passage-tunnels,

into him, and we met there,
in a way that shocked, scared me,

so much I had to lie a while and reflect
upon it, the way we

were freed from ourselves;
joined up.

Trans-earth-Express
For Stevie Smith, died march 7ᵗʰ, 1971

To be barely able to get out of bed this morning
was a great vexation indeed.

It made me plead so very hard
to have control of my nuisance body.

I begged to once more be standing like a warrior
in praise of the golden sunlight.

I wanted it more, much more, because it was restricted,
I wanted it because of my plight.

But then I saw this life I want to consume
as not really mine to be bossing.

I looked out the window and knew how, like a river,
no-one can possess a passing thing.

On a day when time feels short
For Raymond Carver, died 2nd August, 1988

The rhododendron in almost a forest of flowers;
the beach, sky, rocks.

And the food we've had from room-service
here by the window—freshly smoked salmon on
home baked bread, still warm, and the bed I'm lying on
now—polished walnut with a headboard like
curved back wings.

And when we came in from our walk there was a
pigeon in our room, a homing pigeon with a green
band on its leg; it had flown in and was not afraid of us,
and my husband coaxed it back to the outside sill,
lowered down the pane

but it wouldn't fly away, not for a long time, not sure
where to go next; what to do with itself.

Light at sea

The decision seems wrong
as we approach Morecambe.
We left sun so strong
I needed factor 30,
now can't see beyond
the gulls on the prom
for a fog so dense.

I make a joke of it—
today is for being free—
smile back at the woman as she power-walks.

Dad refuses coffee in the Midland,
makes up an excuse about the dog,
so we potter around the indoor market;
pass the man and his jars of sweets,
tell the veg lady how her raspberries
look fantastic.

Then a stroll down the wet beach
to find Brucciani's closed.
On to the old book store,
Books painted huge across a blue wall,
and in goes dad on his current mission—
Step on a Crack—which he finds
(but will not buy) for £5.

I wander along aisles of literature,
taking in the smell,
tall stacks: I'm on a book-ship,
a vessel made only of paper,
words, words everywhere; book-spines
become decking. I breathe print.

Find the poetry. Old greats
Tennyson and Coleridge, dusty
Wordsworth, Keats and,
as if waiting, a hardback text
from another part of the ship,
the title 'I am with you Always',
Holman Hunt's *Light of the World*
on the cover. Bright orange. £3.

Postcard by my window

The Light of the World, *Holman Hunt,*
Keble College chapel, Oxford

Back home, I find the postcard in my case,
prop it on the window ledge,
in a corner by dusty beach-finds.

Nothing more,
until I catch his face, his eyes
in various lights of morning, after rain.

Times when I'm full of words, or haste—
something fine to catch hold of,
some thread hung down in the darkness.

I look at him when the day is fresh
from watching honeybees
around the flowering raspberry,

when I've been kicking molehills with Joseph,
shouting *BOOM!* to all the valley.
When the morning frost lingers

but ducks rise up from the river.
I look at him when I need more than a guide.

Shapeless

after reading 'The Airy Christ', *by Stevie Smith*

You talk about him so bravely.
I envy you that.
Now poems with Jesus in
probably go quick to the 'no' pile.
So how you do inspire me,
talking so freely about him —
the song being much more the gist
than the biography.

He was out of a virgin, perhaps,
and rose from the dead — maybe.
In between this — kind healing, little miracles.
I believe it's possible. Life is magic, after all.

He was special, I see. Very.
But what was the point?
It was the song, we agree.
Love love, hate hate, as you say.
Don't make a fuss
about all the other stuff.

Love deserves an alleluia, yes.
Love deserves astonishment.
More astonishing perhaps than
his bread to wine, his fishes.

That he talked, even went on, even sang
about love with a capital 'L',
yes, Love, I dare it! Why not?
It was his song, like you said,

he wanted this so much for us,
past the wooden crib, the crucifix,
out into the glories of something
we cannot put in a shape,
no matter how we wish we could.

Magic Roundabout

I

Horses with wild manes,
eyes wide as nostrils flare
and the whole machine pulses

with light. Light that is all
the carousel is made of, so bright
it carries the stars like raindrops.

And you, a speck within a speck
of a speck of paint, on the fetlock
hair of one small pony as it spins.

You, an infinitesimal part of this,
carrying the light of the carousel,
radiant.

II

Afraid of losing her happiness
so she made herself blue,
afraid of losing her peace
so she made herself fretful,
afraid of dying
so she made herself hurt.
Catch the devil before the devil catches you!
she thought,
without knowing she was thinking it at all.

III

Let herself imagine:
to be purely happy,
to be completely at peace,
to be so healthy she could run up Criffel mountain,
and the fear of it was what shocked...
To be afraid of bliss? Why?
And she thought she needed a hand to hold,
because to go into that alone
would be too shattering
if it stopped.

But why would it stop?
she asked herself.
Because things do,
she replied.
Things die.

Is that just a lie?
She asked herself again.
Your fear is perhaps not
that bliss might end,
but that you
are not in control of it—
you are not in charge of the carousel,
so you get off,
don't even enjoy the ride.

IV

She climbed slowly back onto the horse
and closed her eyes.

The ladybird, the barn owl,
the squatting frog,

elephant, full belly, snake.
Red apple, rainbow, great oak tree,
lion's-tail, fish-eye, face.

All circular or cylindrical,
the cycle of life embodied,
as moon, sea-wave, icicle,

a swim-stroke, swan's wing-beat,
coming of sun after rain.
We rise, we fall, we rise again

in a universe enclosing this shape:
so with our worship of gods within
all life, to obedience of one abstract judge,

and on with a flight from the patriarch,
spiral now to a reverence of Love.

We sit on Warren Hill and watch the sky

Olber's Paradox asks this:
how come
with an infinity of stars,
the night-sky is still dark?

My favourite answer:
because the universe is young—
as if the sky hasn't realised yet
how light it is.

Finding things at the Exhibition

S
CHI
IHA
LLION

The notice underneath the display
asks visitors not to touch
the artwork:
blocks of wood
engraved each with a letter
in a pyramid shape—

you love it for its senselessness,

start making new words
in your head—
NHALCH,
sounds like old boots
moving through mud,
nhalch….nhalch…nhalch

back to the room, the tour,
excitement nearly popping you—
beginning to find the rabbit amongst the grasses again…

come to the sign on the wall,
discover it is in fact a word,
spelled wrong—
Schiehallion,
a Skye mountain,

some trickster has fiddled with the blocks,
changed 'E' to an 'I'
and no-one knows where 'E' has gone!

Bugs Bunny jumps up from between some wild rhubarb leaves
and you leave, laughing.

How it is
after reading Charles Bukowski

Head numb on these new pills
I pick up your book, look at you,
your sketched face on the front of
COME ON IN!
It makes my evening less screwed
when I move the cover, touch, not dust,
but what could be ash on my fingers,
dropped
          from your cigarette.

Next morning I take a bus to a pretty town,
walk about, your book in my bag,
try to wake up my brain,
or at least get used to it.
I find a 1950's musical box in an antique shop.
Take it down to the field by the lake and
sit
          looking at geese and boats and kids on holiday.

The box plays *Que sera sera*
and although I've only wound it twice
it won't stop, even when I close the lid.
So I leave it open. Let the ballerina dance her little dance.
All the people around me wondering what cloud I'm on.
And the geese, honking.